IMAGES
of America

SWEDES OF GREATER WORCESTER

1889

ÅRS
ALMANACK
UTGIFVEN AF
AMERIKANSKA
EMIGRANT
KOMPANIET

Emigrants from Sweden increased dramatically in the late 1800s, and America was the most popular destination. Several companies were organized to help direct the newcomers to places promoted by land agents eager to sell land. This publication, the *1889 Almanac*, published by the American Emigrant Company, advertises boat and railroad tickets, land in Nebraska, Texas, and California, as well as useful information on American manners and business.

IMAGES
of America

SWEDES OF GREATER WORCESTER

Eric J. Salomonsson,
William O. Hultgren,
and Philip C. Becker

ARCADIA
PUBLISHING

Published by Arcadia Publishing
Charleston, South Carolina

Library of Congress Catalog Card Number: 2002108413

For all general information contact Arcadia Publishing at:
Telephone 843-853-2070
Fax 843-853-0044
E-mail sales@arcadiapublishing.com
For customer service and orders:
Toll-Free 1-888-313-2665

Visit us on the Internet at www.arcadiapublishing.com

Members of the Swedish Folk Dance Club of Worcester pose for a photograph in 1967. From left to right are the following: (front row) Marilyn Johnson, Margaret Larson, Norma Ahlberg, and Margaretha White; (back row) William Hultgren, Carl Larson, musician Lars Kullberg, Kenneth Ahlberg, and James White.

CONTENTS

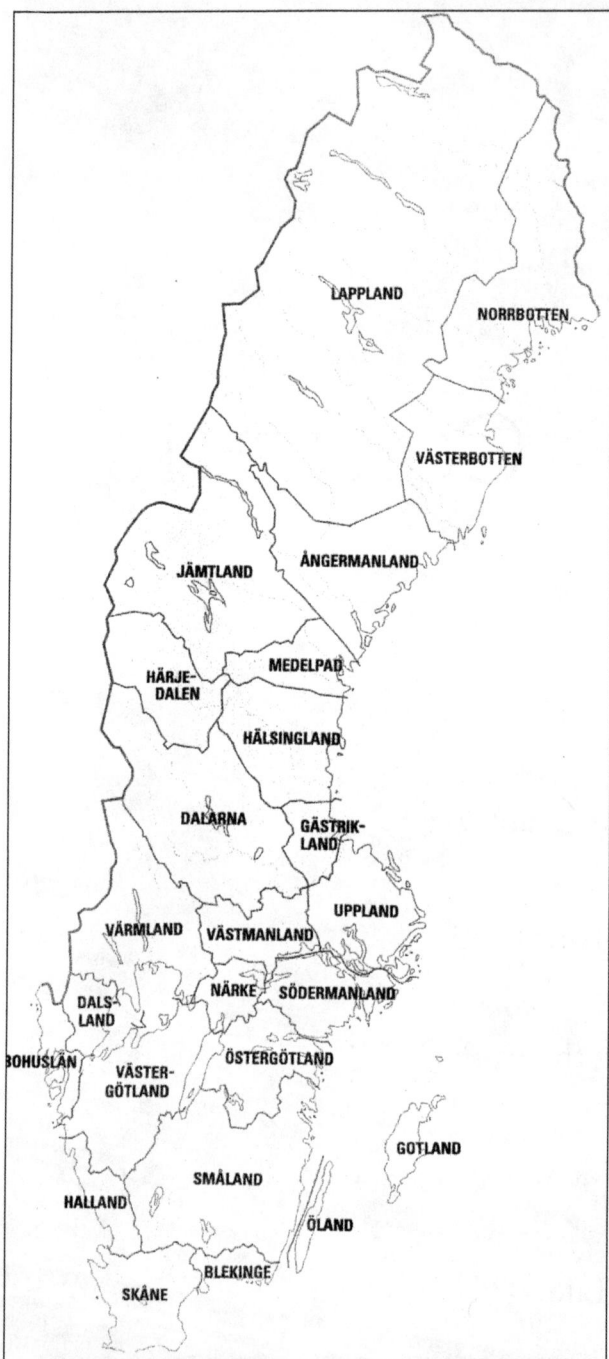

The kingdom of Sweden, with an area of 173,731 square miles (451.701 square kilometers), is the fourth-largest nation in Europe in terms of area, and is similar to the state of California in size. Located in Northern Europe, Sweden is bounded by Norway to the west and the Baltic Sea to the east. In the northeast, it is bounded by Finland. Shown here are the provinces of Sweden. Most Swedes identify themselves by the province from which they came. Hence, one may not only be a Swede, but a *Värmlänning* or a *Skåning*.

INTRODUCTION

When one thinks of the Swedish presence in the United States, one thinks of the upper Midwestern states along the Mississippi River. As strong as the Swedish population is in the states of Minnesota, Illinois, Iowa, and Wisconsin, there is another concentration of Swedes in southern New England. This concentration is largely overlooked by historians in general.

While the Swedes in the Midwest mainly came to take up the rich lands for farming, the New England Swedes came to fill the places of manufacturing and commerce, a few moving out to the countryside, buying older, worn-out Yankee farms.

The largest Swedish community in New England developed in the city of Worcester and the surrounding towns of Worcester County. From a sole Swede in 1868 to 38,000 Swedes and their first-born in 1930, the Swedish element in this area became firmly established in the wire mills, ceramic industry, tool and machine shops, and other professions. By 1930, about one in five people in Worcester were Swedish.

What led so many Swedes to come to Worcester? Crop failures in the latter part of the 1800s, economic hardships, and religious and political unrest led many to come. The letters home, known as the "Amerika brev," extolled the richness and opportunity in America and played an important role in the decision to "gå till Amerika."

During this time, many Swedish-speaking Finns left Finland (then under the control of Russia) to escape conscription in the Russian army or religious and economic persecution. Swedes by heritage, they soon organized their own churches, clubs, and other social organizations. After a time, they melded with the Swedes, thus adding another element in the Nordic heritage throughout the Worcester area.

Iron working and ceramics, jobs long familiar to Swedes, were two of the major industries in Worcester. Yankee, and later Swedish manufacturers, openly recruited Swedes to come and fill the vacancies within these industries, sending agents to Sweden who would even assist with the passage fare if the workers came to Worcester.

The last great famine in Sweden, which occurred during World War I, gave the last impetus to emigrate. Thereafter, the economic situation in Sweden began to improve following the war. Immigration quotas further reduced overall immigration into the United States by the mid-1920s. The last great wave of Swedish immigration occurred in 1923, when almost 25,000 left the country.

Due to the ease with which the Swedish people integrated themselves into the American culture and the similarity of their customs, faith, and work ethic with the Yankee population, their Swedishness rapidly diminished with time. The events of World War II encouraged the transition to "100 percent American" during this period of renewed patriotism. The decline in the use of the Swedish language was hastened, and the idea of remaining socially within the Swedish community came to an end. The last Swedish language church service was held by the Salvation Army during the 1950s, while most of the other 13 Swedish-speaking congregations had moved to English as early as 1928. A Roman Catholic church, St. Catherine of Sweden, was founded in Quinsigamond Village to serve, among others, those Swedes who had married into the Catholic community.

Today, the heritage is present in the celebration of the great Swedish holidays: Midsummer, on the longest day of the year; Sankta Lucia, the celebration of light near the shortest day; and Julotta, or the early Christmas morning church service. Although thoroughly Americanized, the Swedish element in Worcester County is strong yet.

This volume is dedicated to Gladys (Berglund) Landquist. As an avid student, historian, and participant in Worcester's Swedish-American community, she committed herself to family, church, and heritage. She will serve as an example to following generations.

One

THE OLD COUNTRY

This is a typical old-country Swedish home from which many young people began their "Amerika resa," or journey to America. This farmhouse is in the province of Hälsingland.

This unusual photograph from the Swedish city of Söderhamn captures a moment in Swedish history never seen since. World War I resulted in disturbances of all phases of commerce. Agriculture and transportation problems, combined with crop failures, resulted in the last period of famine in Sweden. Nationwide demonstrations occurred, calling for the government to help relieve the nation's suffering. As a result, the Social Democratic Party gained control of Parliament during the 1920s, a reign that continues—with few exceptions—to this day.

The Nordquist family gathered for a photograph at their Hälsingland home a few years before immigrating to Worcester. On the left is Birgitta Nordquist, her daughter Alma Linnea is fifth from the left.

Maria Carlson and her niece Ida Carlson pose for this patriotic portrait before leaving their home in the province of Värmland. The Swedish-Norwegian Union flag and the Stars and Stripes form the background for this domestic scene, which involves the ever-present coffee. In Worcester, Maria married Olof Palm, and Ida married Emil Johnson.

Alma Linnea Nordquist (seated) and her friend Anna are shown in this 1919 photograph in their hometown of Söderhamn in the province of Hälsingland prior to leaving for the United States.

This photograph shows the Zetterlund family homestead in Munkfors, Värmland, Sweden. It was here that Hildur Olivia Zetterlund was born and raised. She married Carl Oscar Franson and immigrated to Worcester in 1910. Shown on the steps are Hildur's daughter Karin (left) and her mother.

Shown here is the schoolhouse in Guldsmedshyttan, Västmanland. Proof of an education was among the necessary papers required of emigrating Swedes. The 1842 law passed by the Swedish Riksdag required each parish to maintain a school, and by the early 20th century the literacy rate in Sweden was nearly 100 percent.

Culinary arts classes were mandatory in the schools, as were general home economics lessons. As a result, many Swedish women became skilled in the art of food preparation, sewing, and knitting. These skills later became valuable in America, where many newly arrived Swedish women became domestic helpers. Shown here is a culinary arts class in Söderhamn.

13

Höganäs is a small coastal town in the province of Skåne. This 1910 photograph shows Höganäs AB, the town's dominant employer. The factory complex lies in the background. John Jeppson and most of Norton's original work force were natives of Höganäs. As president of Norton Company, Jeppson would later construct the Indian Hill Village neighborhood based on the worker's housing shown here in the foreground. (Courtesy of the Höganäs Museum.)

The Dalarna countryside makes for a poignant backdrop in this 1917 photograph showing Signe Salomon (right) and friends adorned in their *folkdräkt*.

For many departing Swedes, the local train station became the scene of sad farewells to both family and friends. For some, it marked the last time they would see their loved ones. Pictured here is the train station in Storå in the province of Västmanland.

Shown here is the Grythyttehed train station in the province of Västmanland. Many of the Worcester-area Swedes came from this province.

This very rare Swedish fraktur death memorial was done by Johan Grundsted in 1884 in memory of Alma Karolina Benjaminsdotter, who died at the age of seven. Folk art such as this is seldom

ᴎᴇ
ᴇʀ
ɴᴀ Bᴇɴᴊᴀᴍɪɴꜱ
ᴇᴋöɴ Vₑₛₜ:ₛ ᴅᴇɴ
ᴅᴇₙ 13:MAJ 1884

AROLINA

Fawel färaldrar od syston kär
till resan jag nu färdig är
Gån wegen rätt till himmelen
så finna ni mig der igen

seen in America. Axel Benjaminsson, brother of Alma, immigrated to Worcester in 1916, taking the name Rydman. His granddaughter is now in possession of this pen-and-ink fraktur.

The forests of Sweden were a ready source of charcoal. In this c. 1890s photograph from Värmland, one can see the technique used in charcoal production. Charcoal was a prime ingredient in the manufacturing of Sweden's high-quality steel. Many men from Värmland immigrated to Worcester and found ready employment in the area's steel mills.

This nostalgic photograph shows Maria Asplund Becker, mother of Karl Petrus Becker, as she reads the newspaper by candlelight at her home in Munkfors, Värmland, c. 1950. Photographs such as this touched the hearts of those who had immigrated to America.

Maria Asplund Becker's avocation was fishing, which was unusual for a woman. She proudly displays her day's catch, likely caught in the Klarälven River in Munkfors, while she was an active octogenarian.

The Swedes' love of music is evident in this late-19th-century photograph. Swedish folk melodies and tunes were passed on at an early age from parents to children. Notice the child with the *dragspel* (accordion). Many of the earliest Swedish social organizations in the Worcester area were musical in nature.

Two

UNTO A NEW LAND

S./S. Hellig Olav.— København — New-York.

The immigrant steamship *Helig Olav* sailed from Copenhagen, Denmark, to New York City with passenger Axel Benjaminsson aboard. He traveled from the home of his youth, Knäred in Småland, to Denmark, where he booked passage for America, sailing on February 27, 1916. On this postcard, which was sent to his brother Carl, he wrote that his room "was as good as any house."

This 1942 postcard shows an aerial view of the Norton Company complex in the Greendale section of Worcester. Swedes at that time made up about half of the work force. John Jeppson, a potter from Höganäs, began producing jugs and crocks for Frank Norton. He was one of a handful of buyers who purchased the grinding wheel portion of Norton's business. Jeppson later perfected the ceramic grinding wheel, and the company rapidly expanded. Eventually, three generations of Jeppsons managed this worldwide corporation. So many workers came from Höganäs that a Höganäs brotherhood was formed, which published its own newspaper.

Axel Rydman (formerly Benjaminsson) is shown here as an employee of the Norton Company. In the previous postcard of the Norton Company, Rydman wrote, "I have worked here 25 years, and it is the first place I worked when I came here."

This 1920s-era Swedish-America Line advertisement shows the liner *Gripsholm*. About one million Swedes immigrated to America between 1860 and 1915 via the traditional route, which brought the immigrants from Sweden to the east-coast English town of Hull. The journey continued by rail to Liverpool, where the "Amerika boats" awaited. The emigration tide steadily increased, and the Swedish-America Line was founded in 1915 to provide direct service from Sweden to America. Following the great period of immigration, the liners were used for luxury pleasure cruises until the Swedish-America Line disbanded in 1975.

Karl Petrus Becker relaxes on the forward deck of an immigrant ship during his initial voyage to America in 1916. After returning to Sweden, he settled in Worcester permanently in 1921.

Through the early morning mist a familiar beacon appears. For many from the decks of the immigrant ships, the first glimpse of the new land was the symbol of America, the Statue of Liberty. This 1916 snapshot was taken by Karl Petrus Becker as he arrived in New York.

Biljett P 11006   Behålles af passageraren.   18-23   3:dje klass

SVENSKA AMERIKA LINIEN
REDERIAKTIEBOLAGET SVERIGE—NORDAMERIKA

Prepaid N:o 11648   Total Amount Paid Dollars 114:73

AXEL H. LAGERGREN, Direktör för Passag.areavdelningen, Drottningtorget 1, GÖTEBORG.

I, Axel H. Lagergren, hereby undertake, upon the following terms, to forward from *Gothenburg* to *Worcester, Mass.* in North America, the emigrant named below for which full payment has been made in America and includes all ordinary charges for landing there.

The journey takes place from *Gothenburg* the 12. MAJ 1921 in the Third class by ocean steamer to *New York* in North America. From New York the Emigrant will be forwarded immediately after having passed the Customs and complied with other formalities, by rail 3rd class to *Worcester, Mass.*

Jag, Axel H. Lagergren, förbinder mig härmed att på sätt här nedan närmare omförmäles från *Göteborg* till *Worcester, Mass.* i Nord-Amerika befordra nedan antecknade utvandrare mot en redan i Amerika till fullo erlagd och härmed kvitterad avgift vari jämväl inräknats de vid landning i Amerika förekommande avgifter av allmän beskaffenhet.

Resan sker från *Göteborg* den 12. MAJ 1921 å mellandäcksplats med ångare till *New York* i Nord-Amerika. Från New York befordras utvandraren genast efter slutad tullexpedition och övriga formaliteter med järnväg i 3:dje klass till *Worcester, Mass.*

Utvandrarens namn	Ålder	Senaste vistelseort
Hilmer Salomonsson	19	Guldsmedshyttan Örebro L.

This May 1921 ticket was issued to 19-year-old Hilmer Salomonsson for his passage from Göteborg, Sweden, to Worcester on the Swedish-America Line. Notice that Hilmer was to travel third class by ship to New York and then first class by rail to Worcester.

Prior to his leaving Guldsmedshyttan in Västmanland to join his brother Carl in Worcester, Hilmer Salomonsson was issued this passport, a necessity for any emigrating Swede. In Worcester, Hilmer eventually Americanized his name to Solomon and married Christine Franson from Munkfors in Värmland. They were the parents of six children.

Fairlawn Hospital, popularly known as the Swedish hospital, employed many new immigrants in various duties. One year after arriving in America, A. Linnea Nordquist and Victoria Bergstrand met their future husbands while working at Fairlawn.

Victoria Bergstrand arrived in Worcester in 1922 at age 22 and began employment as a domestic, a job many young immigrant Swedish women found readily available. Swedish girls were prized for their honesty and hard work. They were also excellent cooks, a trade they acquired through culinary training in Sweden.

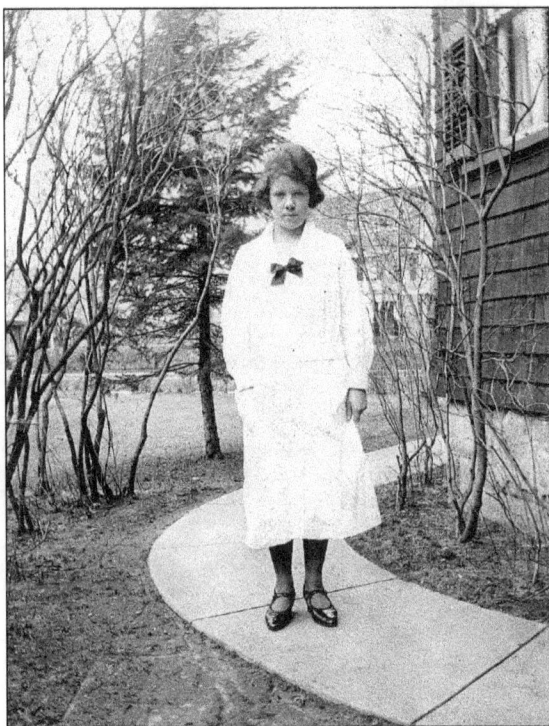

The Nordquist family arrived in Worcester on July 4, 1921, from Hälsingland. Here, the family poses for a 1922 snapshot in the backyard of their home in Worcester. Shown, from left to right, are Birgitta (Nordquist) Peterson, an unidentified person, Doris, Eric, Helge, Linnea, and Göran. The young girl in the front is unidentified.

Many of the working class people lived in the thousands of three-decker homes covering the hills on Worcester's east side. Jennie Rydman was so proud of her apartment at 11 Hooper Street that she sketched a floor plan labeling each room of the apartment and sent it back to Sweden.

Jennie (Persson) Rydman, in her later years, poses in front of her home at 11 Hooper Street.

The Skarin family poses for a portrait in 1900. Shown, from left to right, are Beda, Anna, John, and William. In 1900, the family lived at 20 Stockholm Street in Quinsigamond Village. William later went on to open a florist shop on Greenwood Street, which he eventually sold to Herbert Berg.

Pictured here are Peter Magnus Boch and his wife, Maria Sophia (Peterson), c. 1885. They lived on Home Street and were very active members in the First Swedish Methodist Episcopal Church.

Emma Lundquist of Worcester poses for the camera in her *folkdräkt* (folk dress) *c.* 1898. While in Worcester, she worked for the Nils Björk Company as a milliner. This photograph was taken in the Astrom studio.

Taken in the studio of two Swedish photographers, Flodin and Thyberg, this *c.* 1890 photograph shows Jon and Maria (Medin) Lindegren fashionably dressed in their winter attire. They had arrived from Sweden in the mid-1880s.

Swedish immigrants arriving at Union Station acquired their first impressions of downtown Worcester as they traveled westerly down Front Street towards city hall. The bustle and vitality of a thriving urban center is evident in this 1938 photograph by Bob Wilson. Unfortunately, all of this urban fabric, with the exceptions of the Civil War statue and city hall (seen in the background), disappeared with the opening of the fortress-like Worcester Center Galleria in 1971.

Three

KEEPING THE FAITH

The First Swedish Methodist Episcopal Church at 9 Stebbins Street is shown in this 1928 view. The original one-story church, completed in 1884, proved inadequate as the congregation expanded. In 1893, the building was raised to permit the construction of a first-floor vestry. Door and window elements of the brick portion were copies of those in the mother church in Degerfors, Värmland. Unfortunately, the church was largely destroyed by fire in April 1977.

JUBILEE SOUVENIR
1878 — 1903
OCTOBER 13.

Albert Hallen Ph.D.
1887 1888

Carl A. Cederberg
1884 1887

Otto Anderson
1875 1879

Daniel S. Forlin
1882 1885

Albert Ericson D.D.
1880 1882

Victor Witting
1889 1894

Henry E. Whyman
1894 1902

Francis O. Logren
1902

Konrad R. Hartwig
1894

Pastors of the First Swedish M. E. Church,
Worcester Mass.

The pastors of the First Swedish Methodist Episcopal Church in Quinsigamond Village are
shown on the cover of a 25th anniversary brochure.

This undated photograph is entitled, "Sunday School Class, Quinsigamond Methodist-Episcopal Church taken at Silven home, 15 Carlstad Street, Worcester." Shown, from left to right, are Augusta Johnson, Alice Lindberg, Alma Johnson, Olga Silven, Emma Hammerbeck, John Gullberg, Gertrude Finne, Gertrude Blom, Ida Fredin, and an unidentified woman.

The interior of the Swedish Evangelical Lutheran Gethsemane Church on Mulberry Street in Worcester looked like this during the 1890s. Construction on this church began in 1882 and took four years to complete. Eventually, the congregation erected a new edifice on neighboring Belmont Street, and this building was sold to the Finnish Working Men's Association in 1910. The building is currently being used for religious purposes.

Pastor E.J. Nystrom of the Swedish Evangelical Lutheran Gethsemane Church poses with 20 members of the 1897 confirmation class. In all, 27 people were confirmed in that year. They were Carl Martin Bengtson, Ellen Maria Carlson, Herman Theodore Carlson, Otto Julius Ekwall, Ellen Gunstrom, Carl Gustav Adolf Hammarberg, Theodore Bernhard Hanson, Johanna Allina Harts, Carl Henrikson, Sophia Elizabeth Bylund Hultgren, Hedda Ellengen Johnson, Hilda Sophia Johnson, Johan Petter Johnson, Ernest Mattson, Carl Arcadias Nelson, Hedda Charlotte Nelson, Hildur Ingeborg Nelson, Edwin Olson, Esther Maria Olson, Vetamins Olson, Johan Alfred Petterson, Augusta Wilhelmina Samuelson, Johan Emil Sandberg, Hildegarde Maria Swenson, Olga Elise Swenson, Peter Leonard Swenson, and Hjalmar E. Walberg.

In 1909, as Worcester's first Union Station was being demolished, Pastor John Eckstrom of the Swedish Evangelical Lutheran Gethsemane Church was able to purchase the salvaged granite blocks for about half their value. These blocks were later used in the construction of a new edifice on Belmont Street from 1910 to 1911. During 1917, the name of this house of worship was changed to the First Lutheran Church. In this c. 1930s photograph, exterior repairs are being made to the church. The edifice is now a Roman Catholic church.

P. A. HJELM
1881-1882—1885-1888

PETRUS OSTROM
1882-1885

L. J. KÄLLBERG
1888-1889

J. W. HJERSTROM
1891-1895

AXEL TJERNLUND
1897-1898

C. W. ANDERSON
1898-1908

J. P. ZETTERVALL
1908-1913

E. J. NORDLANDER
1914-1917

A. E. LINDBERG
1918-1928

Shown here are the former pastors of the First Swedish Baptist Church. They served from 1881 to 1928.

Members of the branch Sunday school of the First Swedish Baptist Church of Worcester gather for a photograph in 1930. This school was organized in 1920 to accommodate the growing number of church members living in the Sunderland Road area. In 1924, a small chapel was constructed on Sunderland Road and classes were held there. By 1930, there were eight classes serving over 80 children.

Baraca is an international, interdenominational organization of Bible classes for young men. Here, the Baraca Class of the First Swedish Baptist Church celebrates its second anniversary in 1914. This group sponsored several church events; chief among them was the annual father and son banquet. The name of this church group was eventually changed to the Fellowship Bible Class.

The Reverend Dr. Morris Peterson served at the First Swedish Baptist Church at 29 Belmont Street from 1930 to 1941. Known as an impassioned preacher, he was quoted by the *Worcester Telegram* in 1930 as saying, "Preach the gospel, jolt them a bit, bawl them out, and they'll always come back for more," and "Dignity has no place on the platform when you've got a red hot sermon to put over."

The congregation of the Belmont Street Baptist Church (formerly the First Swedish Baptist Church) poses for a photograph during their 75th anniversary celebration in November 1955. The ornate interior of the church remains in near-original condition as of 2002.

A young men's group of the First Swedish Baptist Church poses with Pastor C.W. Anderson (second row, center) in front of the architecturally impressive front entrance of the recently completed church in this *c.* 1908 photograph.

This 1860 view of Salem Square shows the Salem Square church (left) prior to its remodeling in 1871. This structure was bought by the First Swedish Congregational Church in 1896 and remained until it was determined, during urban renewal, that the building be torn down in 1969 to allow for the construction of the Worcester Center Galleria.

The First Swedish Congregational Church of Worcester was organized in 1880. In January 1885, this edifice on Providence Street was dedicated. It served as the home for the congregation until 1896, when the congregation moved to the Salem Square building.

The 22 members of the First Swedish Congregational Church Band pose for this 1898 photograph.

Pastor O.P. Peterson is surrounded by 39 confirmed candidates from the First Swedish Congregational Church in this 1910 studio photograph. Seen here are, from left to right, the following: (first row) Alma Danielson, Lily Fagerquist, ? Ohrn, and Agda Johnson; (second row) Ida Hulteen, Clara Blomquist, Mabel Brink, Pastor Peterson, Edith Grundstrom, Ruth Thoreen, Ruth Holander, Edith Anderson, and unidentified; (third row) unidentified, Gustaf Nystrom, Paul Allen, Ellen Anderson, unidentified, Hilda Fagerquist, Helen Hagberg, Bertha Olson, unidentified, Ada Anderson, Jenny Bergmark, Anna Ullstrom, unidentified, Axel Westling, and ? Ross; (fourth row) unidentified, Frank Frye, Arthur Peterson, Oscar Anderson, two unidentified boys, Elmer Anderson, unidentified, Melchor Werme, two unidentified boys, and Axel Johnson.

Pastor J.A. Hultman, known as the "Sunshine Singer," is surrounded by the ladies of the Ebenezer Women's Group c. 1901.

The popular Te Deum Male Chorus originated in the Salem Square Congregational Church. From left to right are the following: (front row) Arthur Backgren, two unidentified men, Arthur Peterson, Joel Anderson, Raymond Larson, Herbert Huggare, and Harry Skogsberg; (back row) unidentified, Frithiof Johnson, Sven Ekberg, Andrew Anderson, Frederick Bjurstrom, and Oscar Messier. The group was under the direction of Arthur Peterson.

The 1936 confirmation class of the Salem Square Congregational Church poses for a group portrait. From left to right are the following: (front row) unidentified, Norma (Wiberg) Pearson, Reverend Ericson, Doris (Lundberg) Erickson, and Esther (Anderson) Werme; (middle row) ? Anderson, Albert Larson Jr., Norman Holm, ? Jacobson, Ruth (Peterson) Holbrook, and Doris (Carlson) Pearson; (back row) Clarence Erickson, Lynwood ?, Robert Anderson, Alden Jacobson, Morton Pearson, and Eugene Monterou.

This exceptional view shows the congregation and choir members of the Salem Covenant Church in its old house of worship in Salem Square in downtown Worcester. In 1947, the

This interesting photograph shows the congregation of the Salem Square Congregational Church

congregation affiliated with the Evangelical Mission Covenant Church of America.

gathered in front of their building following Sunday morning service on September 14, 1930.

The Second Swedish Congregational Church at Greenwood and Halmstad Streets started as a mission of the First Swedish Congregational Church in 1892. Both churches were Mission Covenant in origin and, like many Covenant churches in New England, were taken under the wing of the Yankee Congregationalists. The church building was completed in 1899, and the turn-of-the-century view shows a residential structure to its right, later remodeled to become the Greenwood Furniture Company under Wilhelm Forsberg. The church changed its name to the Bethlehem Covenant Church in the late 1940s.

This photograph shows the Bethlehem Covenant Church confirmation class of 1955. From left to right are the following: (front row) Susan Ekstrom, Gail Peterson, Pastor Virgil Wickstrom, Louise Johnson, and Sally Jacobson; (back row) Alan Shrayer, Morton Mattson, Dorothy Keyes, Walter ?, unidentified, William Hultgren, William Johnson, Carol Hanson, and Christopher Borglund.

The Swedish Evangelical Lutheran Emanuel Church was founded in Quinsigamond Village in 1896. Two laymen, Carl Larson and Otto Broberg, had started a Sunday school in 1893 as an outreach of the Swedish Evangelical Lutheran Gethsemane Church. Out of this Sunday school, located in this heavily Swedish neighborhood, grew the Emanuel Lutheran Church. By Christmas morning of 1898, the congregation could assemble in the building for Julotta. Architect Olof Z. Cerwin designed the church in the Gothic style, and it was dedicated on November 10, 1899.

The current Emanuel Lutheran Church, at 200 Greenwood Street, was designed by Arland A. Dirlam of Boston and was dedicated in 1961.

This photograph shows an interior view of the Swedish Evangelical Lutheran Emanuel Church. The large altar painting was removed and reinstalled in the chapel of the new Emanuel Lutheran Church.

Pastor Albert J. Laurell poses with the 1929 confirmation class of Emanuel Lutheran Church. Confirmed that year were Helen Oberg, Carl Sander, Carl Brommels, Svea Bengtson, Helen Fegreus, Edith Lyrberg, Roselia Sjoberg, John Carlson, Herbert Gustafson, Henry Hultquist, Gustaf Holst, John Peterson, Walter Dahlstrom, Mildred Tell, Ethel Anderson, Frances Swenson, Robert Bröte, Elma Anderson, Runo Wahlstrom, Earl Holmes, Fred White, Ellen Anderson, Alice Wigren, and Hanna Willard.

During the pastorate of Rev. Carl B. Sandberg (1915–1923), the use of the "American language" in occasional services appeared for the first time. Upon his resignation to a congregation in Rhode Island, Rev. A.J. Lawson preached. Reverend Lawson would be instrumental in establishing Immanuel Lutheran Church in Holden. Shown here are Reverend Sandberg and his wife.

The Reverend Wallace Cedarleaf poses in this picture with the confirmation class of 1950 at the Chaffin Congregational Church in Holden. From left to right are the following: (first row) Ruth Ann Loff, Ann Belanger, Phyllis Hermanson, and Patricia Hedlund; (second row) Karen Marquist, Linda Maki, Nancy Wood, and Nancy Landgren; (third row) Terrance Nisi, unidentified, James McLain, and Stephen Adams; (fourth row) Charles ?, John ?, Mark ?, and Andrew Reid; (fifth row) Jeffrey Johnson, David Potter, and two unidentified people.

The Chaffin Congregational Church grew rapidly as the town of Holden expanded, doubling its membership between 1950 and 1960. Space was needed in the growing church, and in this 1959 photograph, we see the Reverend Wallace Cedarleaf breaking ground for the new education wing and offices.

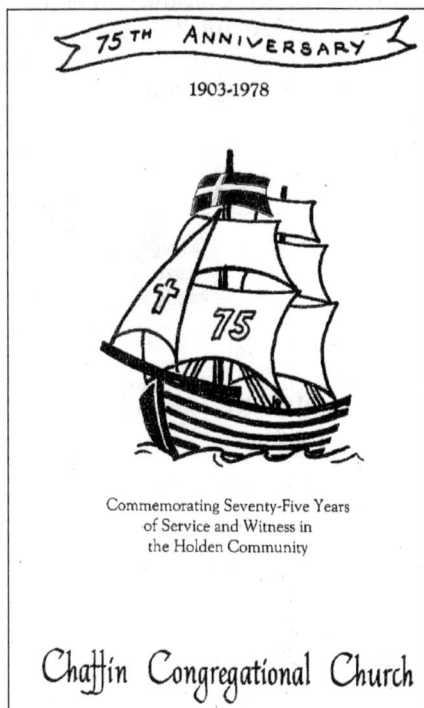

75TH ANNIVERSARY

1903-1978

Commemorating Seventy-Five Years
of Service and Witness in
the Holden Community

Chaffin Congregational Church

The Chaffin Congregational Church produced this booklet for the 75th anniversary in 1978. Notice the use of the ethnic theme, with the Swedish flag flying high on the foremast. A Sunday school, started in 1887, was reorganized in 1892 as the Swedish Christian Workers Association of Chaffin in Holden. Their goal was "to work together in brotherly love to spread the Gospel especially among Scandinavians in Holden." Their Swedish chapel was dedicated in 1895 and, in 1903, society members formed a church called the Scandinavian Evangelical Congregational Church. In 1947, its name was changed to Chaffin Congregational Church.

With the Norton Company attracting an increasing number of Swedes to the Greendale section of Worcester, the need for a Lutheran church became apparent. After several failed attempts, the congregation of the Evangelical Lutheran Zion Church was established on October 21, 1914. Construction of the church began in 1916 and took four years to complete. On July 11, 1920, the Zion Lutheran Church was dedicated. For many years, the edifice was popularly known as the Greendale Lutheran Church. This photograph shows the building shortly after its completion.

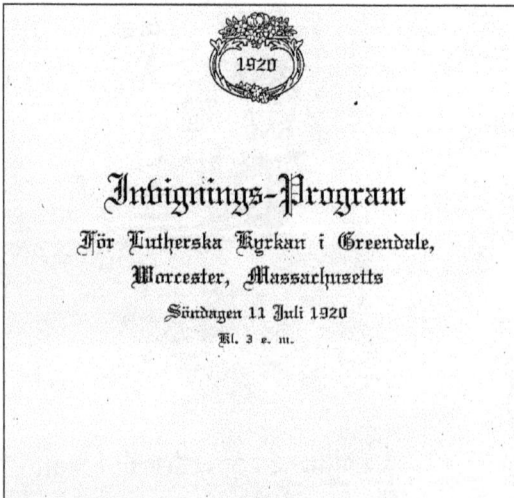

The dedication of the completed Zion Lutheran Church was held on Sunday, July 11, 1920. Shown here is the program book, which was printed in Swedish.

The Second Swedish Methodist Episcopal Church was organized in 1888, purchasing an existing church structure at Thomas and Commercial Streets in Worcester. It quickly became popularly known as the Thomas Street Church. In June 1926, the congregation broke ground for the new Epworth Swedish Methodist Episcopal Church and sold its old building. This structure was subsequently converted into the Peterson-Varg Furniture Company store and later became a victim of urban renewal in the 1960s.

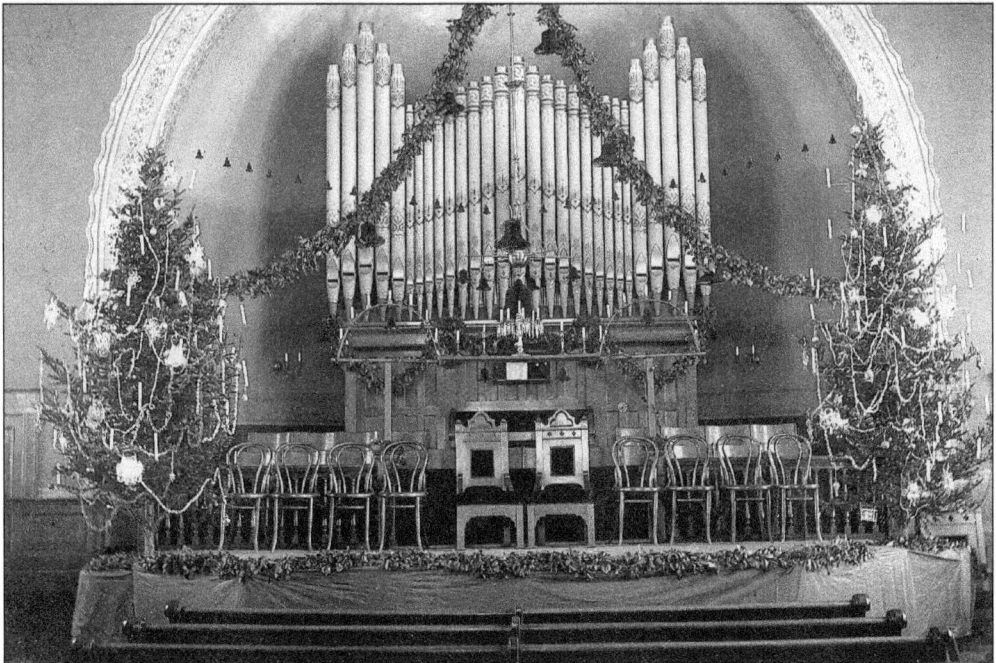

The sanctuary of the Thomas Street Church is decorated for the Christmas season in this unique 1895 photograph.

The charter members of the Second Swedish Methodist Episcopal Church pose for a photograph during the 25th anniversary of the congregation in 1910. Regina and Lars Petterson are in the front row, eighth and ninth from the left.

The Sunday school teachers of the Thomas Street Church gather for a group picture in 1910. Lars Petterson, Sunday school superintendent, is sixth from the left in the back row.

Dedicated in June 1927, the new Epworth Swedish Methodist Episcopal Church at Salisbury and Lancaster Streets was considered to be one of the most attractive of the area's churches. By the time this photograph was taken in 1958, the name had been changed to the Epworth Methodist Church.

Pastor Francis C. Wilson greets parishioners after worship service in the new chapel of the Epworth Methodist Church in Worcester. This chapel was constructed in 1956 and consecrated in 1957.

This September 1924 photograph shows the members of the fledgling Bethel Lutheran parish of Auburn digging the foundation of their church on Bryn Mawr Avenue. Excavation for the edifice began on September 14, and services were held in the completed lower level of the church that Christmas. The entire structure would not be completed, however, until 1929.

Pastor J. Robert Norlander leads the worship service at the Bethel Lutheran Church c. 1955. Reverend Norlander was newly graduated from Augustana Theological Seminary in Illinois when he assumed the pastorate at Bethel Lutheran Church. During the first three years of his 10-year tenure, he doubled the membership of the church.

This drawing, which appeared in a 1949 issue of *Svea* (the Swedish-American newspaper), shows the design of a new Bethel Lutheran Church parish hall and a total remodeling of the original church, as proposed by Swedish architect Martin Hedmark. The parish hall was built in 1950, substantially the same as shown in the rendering. The sanctuary revisions were never carried out, as the parish realized that the aesthetically pleasing exterior would have forced Bethel to live within the footprint of the old building, hampering any possibility for future expansion. It is interesting to note, however, that had the church been built, Auburn might very well have housed one of the most "Swedish" church buildings in the country.

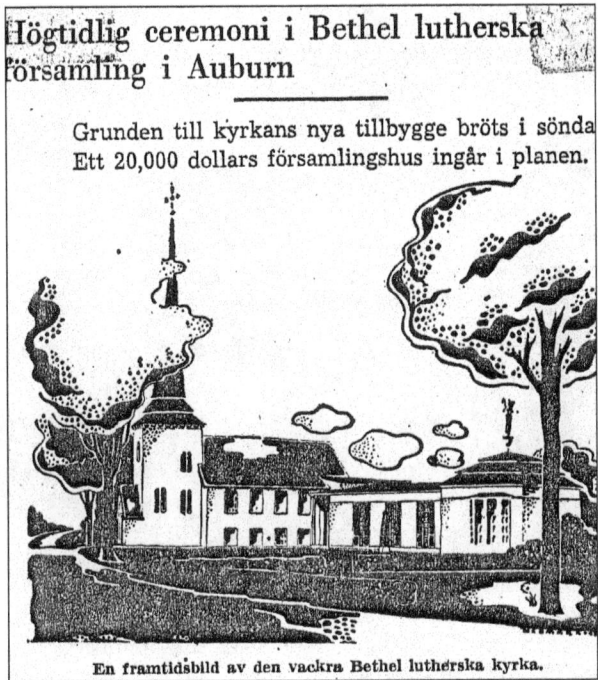

Högtidlig ceremoni i Bethel lutherska församling i Auburn

Grunden till kyrkans nya tillbygge bröts i sönda
Ett 20,000 dollars församlingshus ingår i planen.

En framtidsbild av den vackra Bethel lutherska kyrka.

Shown here is the original Bethel Lutheran Church with the new parish hall. This new hall was dedicated March 5, 1950. The hall was retained when the original church was replaced, but subsequent renovations have altered the once distinctive Swedish architectural traits.

On November 2, 1958, the cornerstone for the current Bethel Lutheran Church was laid. This photograph shows Pastor George W. Schwanenberg, surrounded by dignitaries and parishioners, cementing in the ceremonial stone. The new church was dedicated on August 2, 1959.

The parsonage and parish house of the Calvary Lutheran Church on the corner of Salisbury and Wachusett Streets in Worcester was dedicated in 1925. For more than 20 years this edifice housed the first English-speaking Lutheran congregation in the area. In 1948, when Calvary became part of the new Trinity Lutheran congregation, the building was removed to make way for the Trinity Lutheran Church. The old Calvary Lutheran Church edifice was then rebuilt in Holden as the new Immanuel Lutheran Church.

Shown here is the Calvary Lutheran Church as it appeared at the time of its completion in 1925. Founded in 1921, the congregation met at the Moen Chapel of the Chestnut Street Congregational Church until its new church home was ready for occupancy.

The new Immanuel Lutheran Church building on Shrewsbury Street in Holden, a resurrection of the Calvary Lutheran Church in Worcester, nears completion in the spring of 1949.

In the years following World War I, a large group of Swedes moved into the Chaffins section of Holden. A Swedish congregational society was formed in 1902, but a number of Lutheran families desired a church of their denomination. In 1927, Rev. Axel J. Lawson and his family moved to Holden with the prospects of organizing a Lutheran parish. The first services were held at the home of Mr. and Mrs. C.J. Hultgren on Shrewsbury Street, and in 1928, a congregation was organized. A chapel was erected the following year. This photograph shows the Immanuel Lutheran Chapel shortly after its construction amidst the open farmland.

Rev. Carl O. Bostrom, pastor, and Rev. Dr. B. Julius Hulteen, vice president of the New England Lutheran Conference, pose for the cornerstone laying of the new Immanuel Lutheran Church on November 14, 1948.

The Immanuel Lutheran Church on Shrewsbury Street in Holden is shown as it appeared prior to the addition of the new gymnasium and parish hall. The new church was dedicated on October 9, 1949.

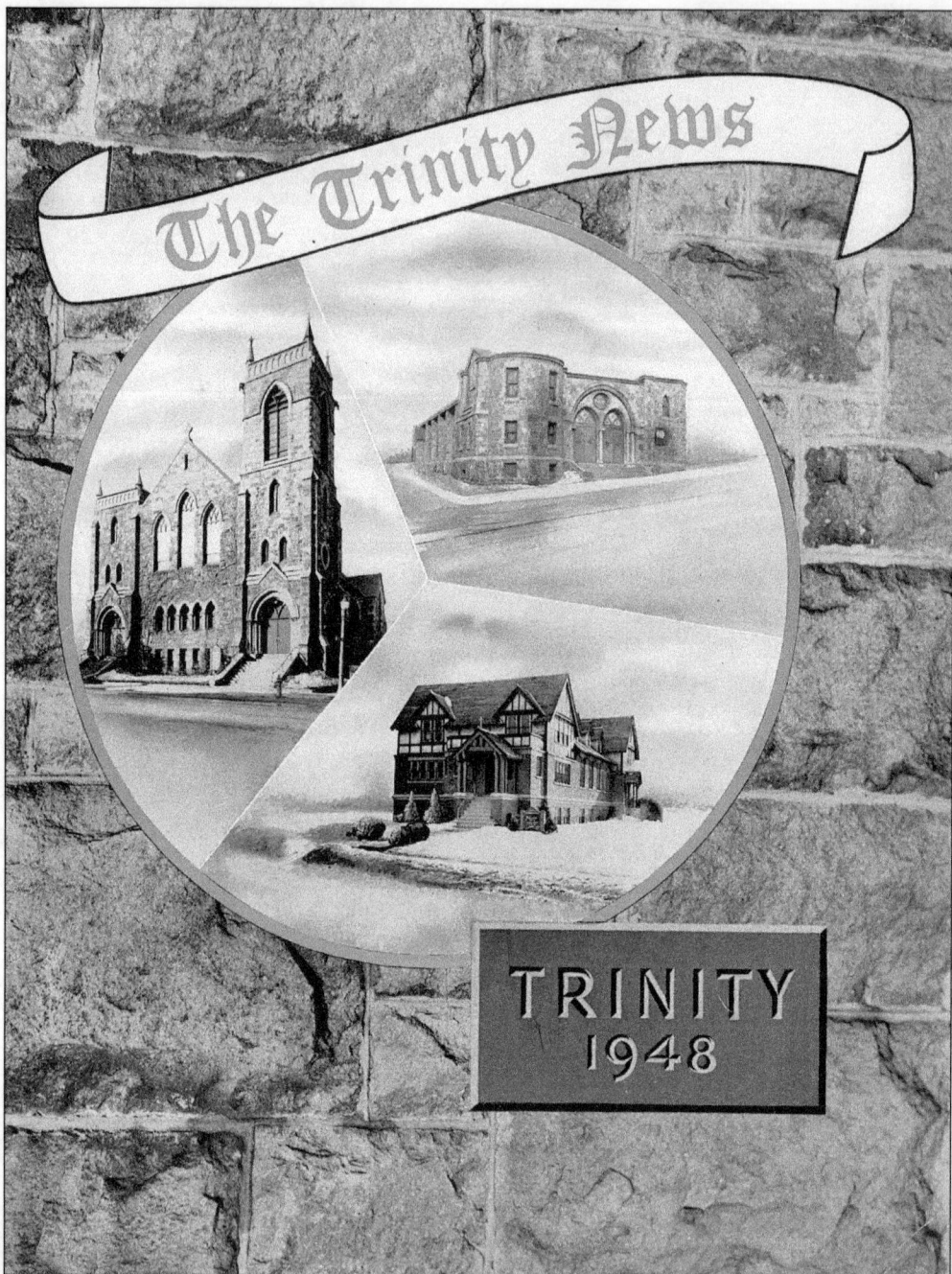

This 1948 cover of *The Trinity News* shows the three churches that merged to form the Trinity Lutheran Church in Worcester on January 1, 1948. Pictured, clockwise from the left, are First Lutheran (Swedish), Bethany Lutheran (Swedish-Finnish), and Calvary Lutheran (English). As the introduction to this magazine states, "In realization of the fact that linguistic distinctions were rapidly becoming a thing of the past, and in further realization of the strength that comes from unity, the three churches voted to become one and build a new church home." That new home was the Trinity Lutheran Church on Lancaster Street, which was dedicated in May 1952.

H. Arnold Barton, the renowned Swedish-American historian, wrote, "Worcester's Trinity Lutheran Church is probably the most faithful replica of traditional Swedish church architecture to be found in America." —*Swedish American Historical Quarterly*.

Pastor O. Karl Olander poses with the 1953 confirmation class of the Trinity Lutheran Church. Those being confirmed that year were Karin Ann Anderson, Karl Siegfried Arndt, Lisa Ann Backstrom, Mildred Marie Benson, Ronald Harold Bjorklund, Tommy Blomfelt, Nancy Marie Bloom, Karen Louise Borg, Norman Iver Carlson, James Bernard Donald, Paul Theodore Englund, Richard Axel Erickson, Allan Roy Fant, Allan Stanley Gustafson, Ann Elizabeth Gustafson, Tanja Hamburger, June Winona Hendrickson, Charles Erik Hoffman, Donna Mae Ingalls, Gustaf Allan Johanson, Joyce Ellen Johnson, Kenneth Gustaf Johnson, Pauline Charlotte Johnson, Virginia Mae Johnson, Walter Harry Johnson, Robert Ralph Kauppila, Robert Clifford Ljunggren, William Francis Menanson Jr., Roger Henry Nettelbladt, Lois Alberta Nilson, Joyce Elaine Okerlund, Brita Ingeborg Sund, Jean Elizabeth Sundlin, John Alf Svenson, Beverly Joann Sweet, Elaine Christine Van Leeuwen, and Rolly Gale Wennerlof.

The collection plate is passed during worship service at the Trinity Lutheran Church in Worcester. This photograph, which dates from the 1950s, highlights the interior architecture of the area's most prestigious Lutheran edifice.

Four

SWEDES AT WORK

In addition to the steel and wire industries, the Morgan Construction Company employed many Swedes. The men in this 1950 photograph are, from left to right, Glen Rich, David Spets, Lars Wennerholm, William Purdy, and Harry Schonbeck.

Höganäs-born brothers John and Peter Carlson arrived in Worcester in 1884 and began working at the Washburn and Moen complex in Quinsigamond Village. Four years after their arrival, they opened up their own store at 133–135 Millbury Street, which specialized in home furnishings. Eventually, Peter left the business and John partnered up with E.T. Rolander to form Carlson-Rolander and Company. Shown here are John (left) and Peter Carlson in an 1898 engraving.

Inspectors played a vital role at the Norton Company. To ensure the highest quality products, special workers inspected the goods prior to shipping. In this 1936 photograph, we see Charles Farr and Harold Hellstrom.

MARBLE AND GRANITE
MONUMENTS.

Oxford, Mass., _Nov. 21_ _1901._

Mrs Lydia A Hall

Bought of OXFORD GRANITE AND MARBLE WORKS,

O. BERGGREN, PROP.

FINE MONUMENT AND BUILDING WORK.

1 Double Headstone $40 00
     Marble

Received Payment.

O. Berggren.

Carl O. Berggren was a stonecutter and quarry man, breaking his own granite from a quarry in Charlton. He and his son were also monument dealers in nearby Oxford.

While the men worked in the fields, the women tended the large vegetable gardens. In this 1925 photograph, Esther Gustafson and her friend Mrs. Nelson admire the Gustafson garden at her home in the Swede Hollow section of Charlton.

Gustaf Sorblom is shown on his Princeton farm in 1937, his horse Chub is pulling a two-horse mower.

A group of Swedes settled in the area of Charlton called Swede Hollow. In this 1941 photograph, Ernest Johnson loads hay into the mow at Meadow Brook Farm on Brookfield Road.

Shown here is Pehr Holger Nelson from Satucket Way in Worcester at work in 1936. Pehr was a vulcanizer—a man who repaired tires.

The Anderson Brothers Dairy was a staple in Quinsigamond Village for generations. Organized in 1903, the dairy was located on Ekman Street. It remained an independent concern until it was bought out in the early 1960s. Unfortunately, this c. 1905 photograph is unidentified.

Svea, the Swedish-American newspaper out of Worcester, was started by Hans Trulson in 1897. It eventually became the largest publication of its kind in the eastern United States and, according to some sources, the largest in the country by 1931. The business eventually expanded into a publication and printing firm, catering to the many Swedish-American organizations throughout the area and beyond. Svea was eventually sold in 1965 and merged with Nordstjernan in New York. Shown here is an advertisement from 1911.

Bertil Westlund relaxes in his office at the Olson Manufacturing Company, which was located on Prescott Street in Worcester and was founded by another Swede, Richard Olson.

Emil Johnson emigrated from the southern Swedish province of Blekinge. He first worked on a farm in Shrewsbury and later at Charlton Depot. Because old Yankee farms were offered for sale at low prices, many Swedes purchased them. Swedish families congregated in communities with their ethnic neighbors. In Charlton, the area around Johnson's farm became known as Swede Hollow for its nearly total Swedish population. One Dane, Mr. Nielsen, was in the minority. Emil Johnson began peddling milk in 8- and 20-quart jugs in Charlton, later using the familiar bottle that can still be found today.

Charles Oslund (bottom), from the province of Gästrikland, arrived in Worcester in 1893. His greatest innovations came in the area of labeling machines, and many of his ideas formed the basis for the modern forms of these machines. In 1914, Emanuel Johnson partnered with Oslund to produce O. & J. labeling machines, which were used throughout the world. The plant was sold to a firm in Chicago following Johnson's death in 1928. Shown here are the two men in a 1917 caricature.

Shown here is the O. & J. Machine Company on 87 Mechanic Street in Worcester, as it appeared in a 1917 caricature.

The Swedish Mercantile Co-op Company at 18–22 Laurel Street was opened in 1883. Reflecting the popular cooperative movement in Scandinavia, this local company helped with the shopping needs of the rapidly expanding Swedish population in Worcester. Here, customers could purchase familiar goods from the old country. In 1909, this building was taken over by F. Wibeck and Company, a Swedish grocery concern. The cooperative eventually moved to 26 Greenwood Street.

Margaret Franson emigrated from Munkfors, Värmland, and arrived in Worcester in 1910. She eventually became a nurse at the Worcester State Hospital before she succumbed to tuberculosis in 1935 at a young age. This photograph shows Margaret (left) and a fellow nurse on the grounds of the hospital c. 1930. In the background stands the impressive Victorian clock tower of the main building.

The employees of the Commonwealth Baking Company at the corner of Arwick and Quinsigamond Avenues in Worcester pose outside of the bakery c. 1920. The business, owned and operated by the Arvidson family, was well known in the area as the maker of Mother's Bread. The business was eventually sold to the J.J. Nissen Company.

Employees of the Commonwealth Baking Company are seen in this 1920 view. Seen here are, from left to right, three unidentified people, John B. Bergdahl, Carl A. Bergdahl, nine unidentified people, Carl A. Bergdahl Sr., Ella Broberg, Carl A. Arvidson, and O. Gustaf Arvidson.

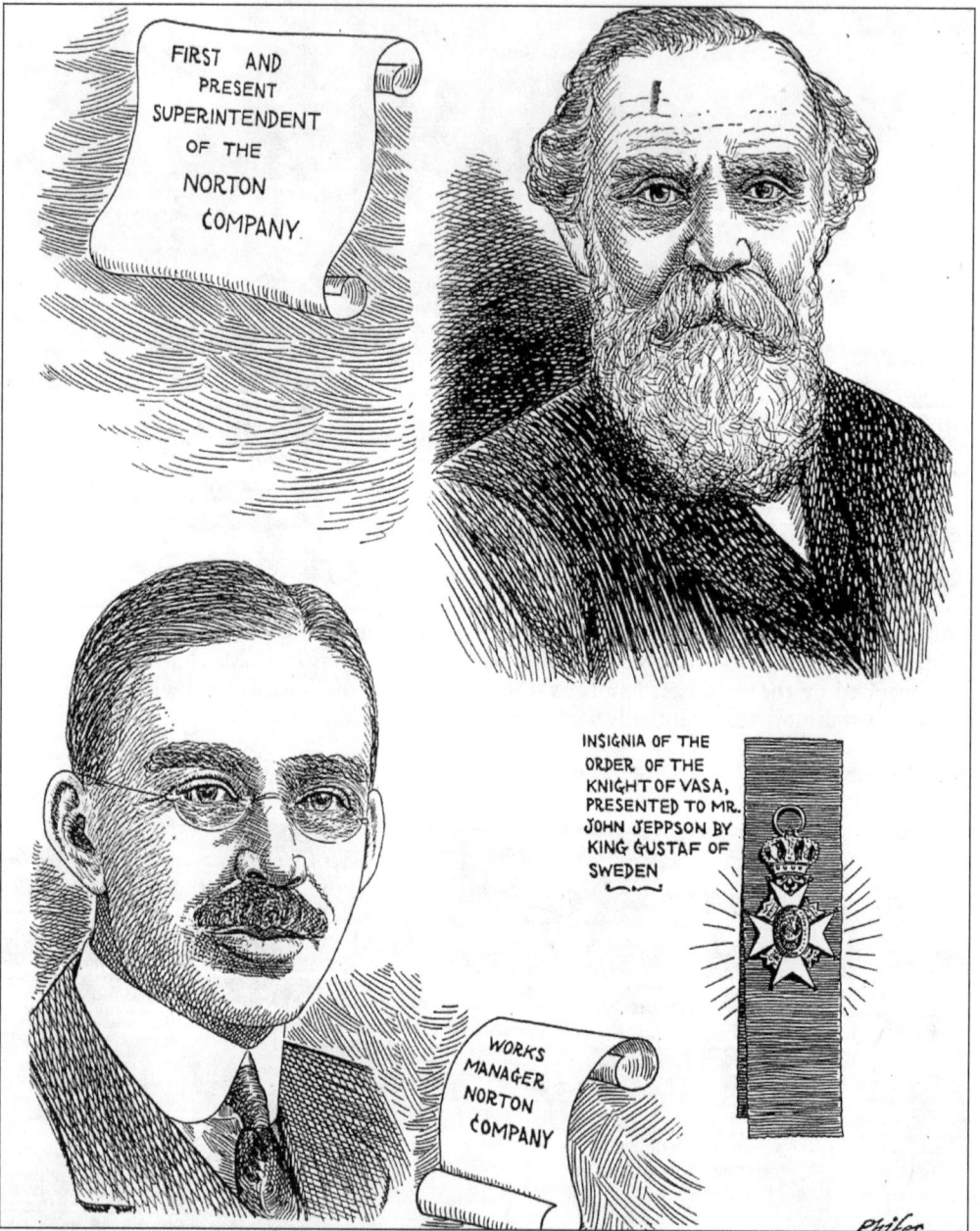

FIRST AND PRESENT SUPERINTENDENT OF THE NORTON COMPANY.

INSIGNIA OF THE ORDER OF THE KNIGHT OF VASA, PRESENTED TO MR. JOHN JEPPSON BY KING GUSTAF OF SWEDEN

WORKS MANAGER NORTON COMPANY

Phifer

The name Jeppson is legendary throughout the Worcester area. Having arrived in Worcester from Höganäs, Skåne, in 1869, Jeppson had become one of the most successful Swedish-Americans in the area by 1900. His greatest legacy was the success of the Norton Company, which he helped mold into a worldwide corporation. Through the efforts of John, and later his son George, the Jeppson family was also one of the largest contributors to the local Swedish-American community. Their gifts included the purchase of the estate that became the Lutheran Home and the money for a subsequent addition, financial support for chapels at the Zion Lutheran and Trinity Lutheran churches, and money for the erection of the Eagle Memorial in Greendale, which was sculpted by the renowned Carl Milles. John Jeppson and his son George are shown here in caricatures drawn in 1917.

This photograph shows a general view of the Norton Company c. 1925.

NEW BOND STREET, THE "MAIN STREET" AND ENTRANCE
TO THE NORTON COMPANY OFFICES AND FACTORIES

Pictured here is part of the Norton Company complex on New Bond Street. The building at the left shows the familiar beehive kilns of the kiln facility. The structure to the right of the kilns housed the corporation's executive offices. This bustling industry was one of Worcester's largest employers and a magnet for thousands of Swedes.

SKANDIA BANK & TRUST

The Skandia Credit Union was organized in 1915 by a group of local Swedish businessmen intent upon helping fellow Scandinavians purchase homes of their own. So successful was the operation that it soon became the largest credit union of its kind in the United States. In 1930, the institution was granted a banking charter by the state of Massachusetts and became the Skandia Bank and Trust Company, later changing its name to Guarantee Bank and Trust. For generations, the symbol of the bank was the Viking ship.

John E. Johnson of Worcester was one local Swede who invested in the fledgling Skandia Credit Union. Here, we see a receipt acknowledging his purchase of 100 shares in 1919.

Two satisfied customers leave the Crown Bakery c. 1964. Borje F. Jalar, president of Astra Pharmaceutical Inc. in Worcester, longed for a taste of the old country and decided to do something about it. The net result was the formation of the Crown Bakery in 1960. Currently owned by Swedish-born baker Jon Lundstrom, the Crown Bakery is known for its outstanding quality and is consistently rated the area's best bakery in local opinion polls.

Swedish Modern
DRIVE IN Bakery

DEDICATED TO PREMIUM QUALITY

we specialize in such Swedish favorites as:

ÄKTA SVENSKA LIMPOR — KAVRING
SVENSKT KAFFEBRÖD OCH ALLA
SORTERS KAKOR — TÅRTOR —
KROKANER — BAKELSER — MAZARINER

The Crown Bakery
Gold Star Boulevard, Worcester, Mass.
Routes 12 and 110   Tel. SW 1-1746

Here we see an early Crown Bakery advertisement from the 1963 edition of *Almanack För Svensk-Amerika.*

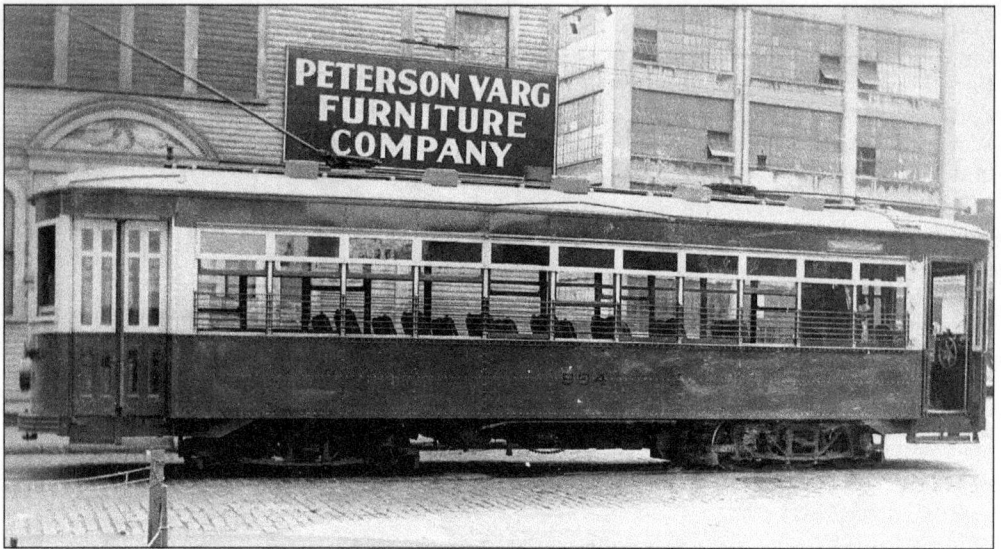

The Peterson-Varg Furniture Company is shown in the background of this 1940s view of Thomas Street at Commercial Street. The building was the old Thomas Street Swedish Methodist Church, vacated in 1926 for a move to the new Epworth church edifice at Salisbury and Lancaster Streets. The business was established by C. Edward Peterson and Philip Varg on April 1, 1927. By 1948, they had moved to 695 Main Street, where they remained until 1953.

We Are Continuing Our

11th Anniversary

With a host of Birthday Values as a part of our 11th Anniversary

—SALE—

Special for This Week

PHILIP H. VARG

C. EDWARD PETERSON

BALLOON CHAIR **$16.50**
Regular $24.50 value

MAPLE
BREAKFAST SET **$14.50**
4 Chairs and Table. Reg. $20.00

10% TO 25% OFF REGULAR MERCHANDISE DURING THE REMAINDER OF THIS SALE.

Peterson-Varg Furniture Co.

Prices were reasonable in this 1938 advertisement of the Peterson-Varg Furniture Company in the *Worcester Evening Post.*

82

This 1948 view shows the Paramount Oilless Bearing Company at 99 Hope Avenue, organized by C. Russell Johnson in 1929. Now known as POBCO, the business is still operated by descendants of the original owner.

In its heyday, Norton Company was a model for the paternalistic relationship it had with its workers. The corporation sponsored athletic teams, Christmas parties with complimentary turkeys, family days, and, as this 1935 photo shows, even carnivals were held during the summer months on the athletic fields.

Andrew P. Lundborg arrived in Worcester from Minnesota in January 1889 and quickly established A.P. Lundborg and Company, which sold such articles as silverware, jewelry, stationery, as well as Swedish-related merchandise. By 1900, he had the largest Swedish bookstore east of Chicago. Here, we see Mr. Lundborg (center), his hands on his hips, posing with employees outside of his store at 221 Main Street in 1898.

Lundborg & Co., Inc.

Jewelry - Watches - Diamonds - Clocks - Silverware

Stationery - Fountain Pens - Greeting Cards
Swedish Imported Goods

288 Main Street

Worcester, Massachusetts January 16th, 1940.

Sold to Miss Anna Erickson, Worcester, Mass.

1 solid gold brooch,
taking out red stone and soldering
on V.O. emblem $5.00

RECEIVED PAYMENT

JAN 17 1940

Lundborg & Co., Inc.

Per ....

Thank you.

Apparently, Anna Erickson held the Vasa Order in high regard. In 1940, she had her solid gold broach refitted with the emblem of the order. The work was done at A.P. Lundborg and Company, a local business that catered to the area's Swedish-American community.

Oscar Lindquist poses in front of his funeral parlor at 11–13 Green Street in Worcester. Lindquist came to Worcester from Uttersberg, Västmanland, and established his business in 1899. In 1915, he moved the funeral parlor to his residence at 36 Butler Street, where it remains to this day.

This 1930s photograph shows Oscar Lindquist with his two grandsons, Stanley Otter (left) and Walter Lundin (right). The grandsons eventually became joint owners of the business.

One of Worcester's largest machine shops was the Heald Machine Company. Founded in 1826, the company located to New Bond Street in the Greendale section of Worcester, directly opposite the Norton Company. This precision grinding and bearing company employed many Swedes among their 3,600 World War II workers.

The Heald Machine Company was converted to wartime production beginning in 1941. In this September 1942 issue of the *Heald Herald*, Wat Tyler Culverius, a naval rear admiral, awards the Army-Navy E pins to the five longest service employees. Shown here are, from left to right, Peter T. Bonn, John A. Christianson, Ernest "Gus" Nystrom, Noah W. Long, and Gustaf L. Hellstrom.

The Washburn and Moen Company was established in 1831 on Grove Street in Worcester. In 1846, the company opened a factory in Quinsigamond Village. The advent of barbed wire fencing on the farms of the Great Plains, coupled with the need for wire to support hoop skirts, allowed Washburn and Moen to expand their business. Having seen firsthand the quality of the Swedish steel and the experience of their Swedish work force, Philip Moen was sent to Sweden to learn the techniques of the iron industry. The Washburn and Moen Company encouraged the immigration of Swedish workers, often hiring Swedes in Worcester to return to the old country and recruit workers for their mills. Thousands of Swedes found their first jobs as employees at the Washburn and Moen mills. Shown here are the North Works; many Swedes from the Belmont Hill area of Worcester were employed in this complex.

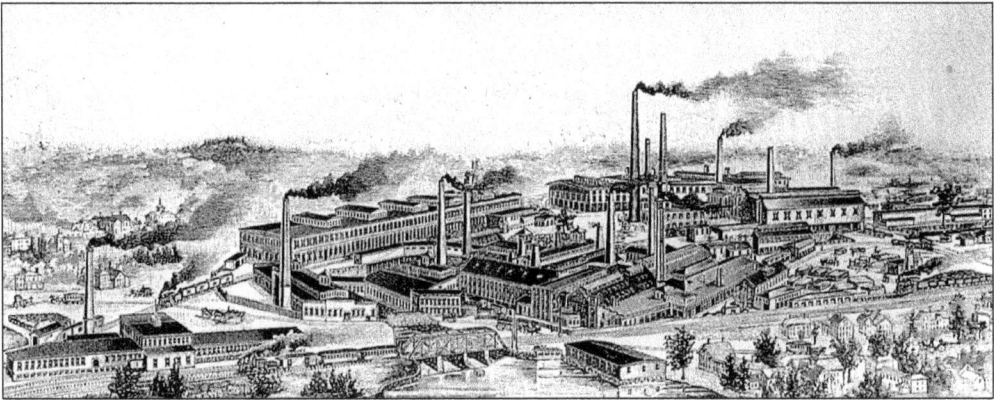

Pictured here is the South Works of the Washburn and Moen Company in Quinsigamond Village. Eventually, an entire Swedish community would develop around this complex.

Litet bo jag sätta vill,
Gård med trädgårdstäppa till;
Och då får jag bästa priset —
Det har ofta mig bevisats —
Utav Sjödin i Fairlawn,
Endast en mil ifrån sta'n.

JOHN G. SJODIN

Contractor, Builder and
Developer
FAIRLAWN CIRCLE
SHREWSBURY, - MASS.
Tel Park 2674

In 1927, John G. Sjodin, a Swedish house builder from Shrewsbury, advertised his contracting business rather ingeniously, including a catchy little Swedish poem, along with a photograph of his handiwork. Loosely translated, the poem reads as follows:

A little house I dearly want,
A yard and garden too.
And when I find a price to suit-
Which often times finds true-
From Sjodin in Fairlawn,
Just one short mile from you.

Herbert Berg became an avid gardener at an early age and, by the 1930s, had established a successful florist shop on Millbury Street in Quinsigamond Village, a business he operated for more than 50 years. The shop is currently operating under new management.

The number of Swedes had increased dramatically in Worcester, allowing the existence of Swedish businesses—places where one could shop and conduct business affairs in Swedish. In this 1907 advertisement, Edstrand and Peterson sold hats, coats, and blouses; C. Nelson's grocery store on Perry Avenue had two branches, where they "constantly had on hand Swedish delicacies;" Messler Photo Studio offered "photos and frames at low prices;" and R.A. Pearson, proprietor of commercial print, offered wedding invitations and calling cards, along with business and club printing.

DR. OSCAR SVENSON
SVENSK TANDLÄKARE
207 MAIN STREET, WORCESTER.
Utexaminerad från Philadelphia Den-
tal College and Hospital of Oral
Surgery.
Telefon 1516—12.

Many of the Swedish immigrants earned their
professional degrees when they came to America.
Dr. Oscar Swenson proudly advertised that
he was a graduate of the Philadelphia Dental
College and Hospital of Oral Surgery. Upon
returning to Worcester, Dr. Swenson had a busy
practice among his countrymen in the city.

Roland Erickson was president of the Guarantee
Bank and Trust Company of Worcester between 1947
and 1964. He also served on the city's chamber of
commerce, Community Chest, and was a director of
the Swedish Cemetery Corporation. In the 1980s,
he headed the Swedish Council of America, the
national umbrella association for the country's
Swedish-American organizations. In 1976, Erickson
was knighted by Sweden's King Carl XVI Gustaf in
ceremonies held at the Swedish Consulate in New York.

90

Lars Petterson, one of Worcester's early building contractors, began his business in 1886. He employed carpenters, stonemasons, plasterers, and painters in his extensive building operations, which included the construction of hundreds of the three-deckers that now dot the Worcester landscape. In this 1909 photograph, Petterson poses with his construction crew at work on such a three-decker. His son Wallace sits in the foreground on a pail.

Swedish ingenuity spawned many small enterprises. The Sjogren Tool and Machine Company was located on Sword Street in Auburn and was one such local shop. Oscar Sjogren was born in Sweden in 1880 and came to the Worcester area in 1902. His shop was family owned and operated by Oscar and his five sons. Founded in 1928, the company manufactured wire supplies and steel and wire products.

Robinson & Anderson, Juvelerare och Silfversmeder, 385 Main St.

Hultman Pianon

Bättre än någonsin. Billigare än tillförne. Begär vår katalog och nya prislista.

J. A. Hultman, 44 Front Street.

Anderson, Borg & Swenson, Clothing and Gent's Furnishings, 21 Thomas Street.

Also Custom Department.   Telephone 5335.

Två butiker.   Sju afdelningar.

Skor, Herrekiperingsartiklar, Juve'erarevaror, Musikinstrument, Pappershandel, Taflor och Ramar, Tvål och Parfymer.

Carl J. Ekstedt, 229-231 MAIN ST.

This 1907 booklet advertises a variety of Swedish entrepreneurs. Robinson and Anderson were jewelers on Main Street. J.A. Hultman, a famous preacher and singer, had a piano and music store on Front Street. Anderson, Borg, and Swenson were on Thomas Street, and Carl J. Ekstedt had two apparel shops on Main Street.

Five

FAMILY LIFE

The first-generation Swedish pursued an education that their fathers thought impossible in the old country. Here, a relaxed Carl Rydman, a graduate of Worcester Polytechnic Institute, reads a 1941 issue of *National Geographic*.

Christine (Franson) Solomon feeds her newborn son, Thurston, in this 1929 photograph taken at her parent's home on Wildwood Avenue in Worcester. The wheels of the baby carriage are still in Thurston's possession. Christine was born in Munkfors, Värmland, in 1909. She immigrated to the United States with her parents, Carl O. and Hildur Franson, arriving in Worcester as an infant in 1910.

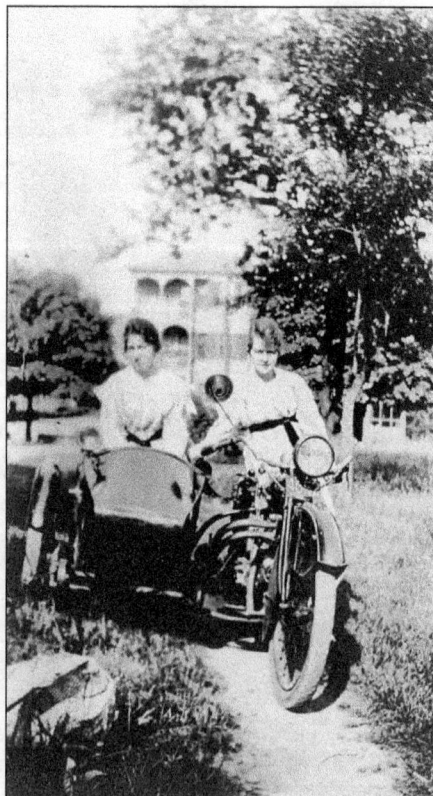

In the days before World War I, it was bold for a woman to drive. Risking public censure, motorcycle driver Signe Clason is shown giving her sister Agnes a ride near their home in the Greendale section of Worcester.

This interior view shows the parlor of Axel and Jennie Rydman's apartment on Hooper Street in Worcester, revealing its mixed uses and décor. Their daughter Helen is on the bed.

Not all wedding dresses were white. Here, the portrait of Mr. and Mrs. Erik Westlund, taken in Worcester, shows dark wedding attire very much in the old-country style.

Dressed in their best apparel for this 1909 photograph are, from left to right, siblings Celia, Thelma, and Frank Bottcher.

Hilmer Solomon must have trusted his friend Edward "Eddie" Hellstrom very much with that straight razor. This 1920s photograph was taken at the Peterson farm in Holden.

Dagny (Sohlman) Johnson, first row, third from the left, poses with her 1923 class at the Trowbridgeville School on Webster Street in Worcester. Dagny was a student in the Swedish Sunday school conducted at this location by Mrs. Walfred Johnson in the 1920s and 1930s.

The Trowbridgeville School was erected by the city of Worcester in 1896 to serve this southwest district of the city. Classes were held until 1932, when it was closed and replaced with the Heard Street School. A branch Swedish Sunday school was held here to serve the area's Swedish residents, as well as those Swedes in neighboring Auburn. The vacant school was purchased by the Swedish Cemetery Corporation, which demolished the structure in 1948.

The envelope company, Logan, Swift, and Brigham sponsored a baseball team, as seen in this *c.* 1910 photograph. Gustaf F. Hultgren poses with his teammates.

Gerda, Helen, and Carl Rydman enjoy sledding at a friend's house in the Norton Company village of Indian Hill.

A stylishly dressed Nancy Clason poses for this
c. 1912 photograph.

Whole neighborhoods were made up of the
popular three-decker houses. This typical
Worcester house at 47 Upsala Street in the
heavily Swedish Vernon Hill neighborhood
was home to the newly married Sorblom family
in 1938: Gustav, Ida, and baby Beverly.

These three bathing beauties, Agnes (left) and Walborg Clason (center) and cousin Esther Hultgren, enjoy a dip, never getting their hats wet, in this 1927 photograph.

These fashionably dressed and hatted ladies, Esther (Monson) Westlund (left) and Anna (Monson) Johnson, pose for the camera in 1908.

Carl G. Westlund built for his family the first house on the street he developed—Westlund Avenue in Auburn.

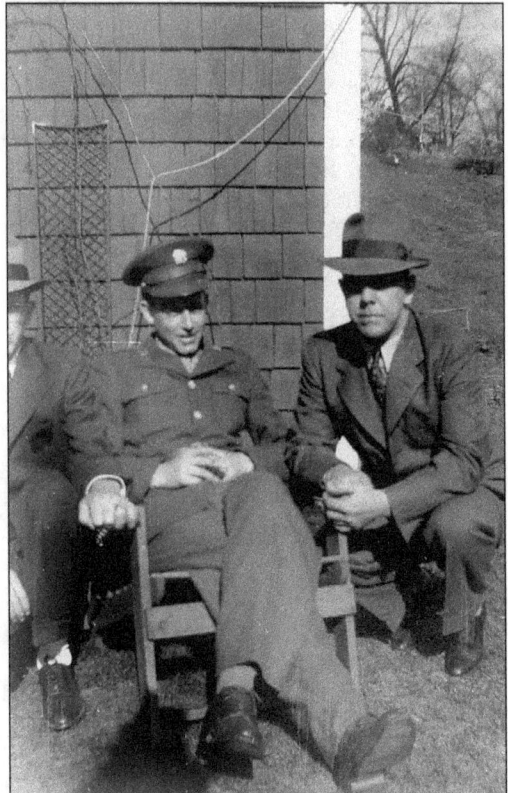

After World War II, Bertil Westlund enjoyed a quiet welcome with his cousin Carl V. Nordstrom at the Westland home in Auburn.

The Bottcher family poses in their home on Holden Street in Holden during the 1930s. Seen here are, from left to right, as follows: (front row) Greda, Elsa, Carl Gotthard, Karin, Irving, Mia, and Elizabeth; (back row) Gurly, Gustaf, Malte, and Henry. Carl Gustaf was born in Helsingborg in 1873 and eventually immigrated to the Worcester area. He started his successful painting business in 1904 and was well known throughout the county. Eventually, several members of the Bottcher family would start up painting businesses of their own, many of which continue to this day.

The two Hultgren families, originally from Hoahult in Västergötland, moved into twin houses on Whipple Street in Quinsigamond Village. These dwellings are seen here c. 1910.

Brothers Gustaf and Walter Wickstrom of 56 Holden Street in Worcester served in World War I. Gustaf served two years in the U.S. Navy on the USS *Bridgeport* and was discharged in August 1919. Walter was a member of the Ordinance Corps and enlisted in December 1917. He served for a year before being discharged in December 1918. Both brothers were members of the First Swedish Baptist congregation.

Beverly, Sandra, and Roy Sorblom are ready to go in their Sunday best in this 1945 snapshot taken in Princeton.

Fellow Swedes gather at Wray Square in Quinsigamond Village for a group photograph in 1943. Seen here are, from left to right, seamen Bill Lawson, Eric Johnson, Paul Wennerstrand, Charlie Brady, and Carl Engvall. In the foreground is soldier Helge Nordstrom. Perhaps these neighborhood friends were on leave when this picture was taken.

The three-decker house is the common house style on Worcester's east side. Here we see Gustaf Hultgren and family caught outside their home at 120 Rodney Street c. 1922.

The rocking horse is close to the real thing. Ida enjoys her toy horse under the eye of her watchful father, C.J. Hultgren, at their farm in Holden in 1919.

Sven and Alice Carlson are shown in this c. 1940s photograph. Sven emigrated from Sweden in 1929 and initially settled with relatives in Palmer. Eventually, Sven met and married Alice Tiderman from Quinsigamond Village. Alice went on to national prominence in Swedish-American affairs, which resulted in her being chosen Swedish-American of the Year in 1987. The ceremonies marking this honor took place in Sweden and included an audience with King Carl XVI Gustaf.

The Quinsigamond Village schoolhouse reflected the heavily Swedish character of the neighborhood. Photographed in October 1930, the students seen here are, from left to right, as follows: (front row) Dorothy Peterson, Frances Nordgren, unidentified, Eunice Becklund, Ingrid Anderson, Ellen Kominsky, Dorothy Jacobson, Helen Olson, and an unidentified student; (middle row) unidentified, Philip Larson, Herbert Gustafson, Stina Peterson, Gerda Anderson, ?, Marion Madsen, Burton Spongberg, Alan Sternlof, Paul Skogsberg, and William Brown; (back row) Richard Forsberg, Herbert Berg, Milton Anderson, Eva Benwood, Lola Wigiert, Jane Davis, Elizabeth Porath, two unidentified students, and Carl Werme.

Ernest and Wilbur Johnson pause on the running board of Elliot Olson's car in this 1917 snapshot at the Johnson farm in Charlton.

Six

PEOPLE AND EVENTS

In this c. 1940s photograph, members of the Swedish Folk Dance Club, walking arm in arm, display their enthusiasm at the end of a Midsummer celebration at Scandinavian Athletic Club (SAC) Park in Shrewsbury. With their Swedish and American flags blowing in the wind, these club members capture the essence of a bygone era. Seen here are, from left to right, Edna Thompson, Yngve Greenlund, Ingrid Osted Anderson, Gladys Berglund, Harold Hanson, and Verner Kullenberg.

Worcester Evening Post

Associated Press — Wide World Photos
Newspaper Enterprise Association Service

WORCESTER MASS., TUESDAY MAY 31, 1938

The History of the Swedish People in Worcester and Worcester County

Commemorating 300 Years of Outstanding Achievement

FAIRLAWN HOSPITAL

LINCOLN AID ASSOCIATION

CONGRESSMAN
PEHR G. HOLMES

GEO. N. JEPPSON

REV. DR. JOHN A. ECKSTROM
Pastor First Lutheran Church
Dean Worc. Swedish Clergymen

SWEDISH LUTHERAN OLD PEOPLES HOME

KAMPEN LODGE I.O.G.T Summer Qu. SEARS Is.

In commemoration of the tercentenary of the founding of the first Swedish colony in America on the Delaware River, the *Worcester Evening Post* issued a 20-page special edition dedicated entirely to "The History of the Swedish in Worcester and Worcester County," highlighting history, notables, businesses, and organizations. The front cover is reproduced here.

July 11, 1938, marked a high point in Worcester's tercentenary celebrations. On that day, Prince Bertil of Sweden arrived for a day of festivities, which included a visit to the Worcester Art Museum. Here, we see the prince (left) seated next to his host, George Jeppson.

RECEIVED

JUN 24 1938   TO MEET HIS ROYAL HIGHNESS

Mayor's Office PRINCE BERTIL OF SWEDEN

The Worcester Tercentenary Committee

REQUESTS THE PLEASURE OF

Hon. William A. Bennett

COMPANY AT LUNCHEON

ON MONDAY THE ELEVENTH OF JULY

AT ONE-THIRTY O'CLOCK

WORCESTER COUNTRY CLUB

Mayor William Bennett of Worcester was invited to attend the luncheon at the Worcester Country Club in honor of Prince Bertil. As one can see, the mayor readily accepted. The mayor presented the prince with a key to the city in the ceremonies at city hall.

In 1938, Swedish-American communities throughout the country celebrated the 300th anniversary of the founding of New Sweden along the Delaware River. On June 5, the sights and sounds of Sweden filled the Worcester Memorial Auditorium and delighted the hundreds who attended. Here, under the American and Swedish flags, is the children's choir of the First Lutheran Church in performance on that historic evening.

The Skandinavisk Idrottsklubb was founded in 1923 and soon became known by its English name, the Scandinavian Athletic Club. In 1928, land was purchased on Lake Street in Shrewsbury, and work soon began on the construction of athletic fields. As is evident in this photograph, the construction of these fields was done by hand, a grueling day's work for those members. Today, the club facilities, popularly known as SAC Park, include a clubhouse that was constructed in 1929. Events ranging from car shows to weddings are held there.

110

Worcester was a popular destination for Swedish and Swedish-American performers. One such entertainer was *Olle i Skratthult* (Olle in Laughterland), who brought his vaudeville show to Tuckerman Hall in February 1928. Swedish-born Hjalmar Peterson was well known throughout Swedish-America, recording numerous comedic songs and ballads. His rendition of *Nikolina* sold well over 100,000 recordings, which was quite impressive for an ethnic-based performer. Shown here in a studio photograph are *Olle i Skratthult* (right) and musician Gustav Nyberg.

Music constituted a large part of Swedish family life. Whether in the home or at a gathering, someone always seemed to have a musical instrument on hand. Here, two accordionists entertain at a gathering of friends during the 1920s.

Members of the Scandinavian Women's Gymnastics Club show off their athletic prowess in this July 1941 photograph taken at the Edgemere Lodge in Shrewsbury. Seen here are, from left to right, as follows: (bottom) Vivian A. Hedquist, Alice G. Johnson, and Liv Lunde; (middle) Doris V. Carlson and Dora A. Frostholm; (top) Evelyn J. Benson.

Fairlawn Hospital was founded in 1921 by a group of Scandinavian-Americans acting on a proposal by the Swedish National Federation. Initially, it had 38 beds, and following alterations between 1936 and 1938 and additions constructed in 1951, 1963, and 1970, it became a 104-bed facility. After 65 years as a general medical-surgical hospital, it became an active rehabilitation facility and still serves the community in this purpose.

The annual doll contest was a much-anticipated event in Quinsigamond Village. Here, we see cousins Ruth and Elizabeth Norling among the participants. Ruth stands on the left in the front row, and Elizabeth is fifth from the left in the back row. The photograph was taken in 1925 in front of the Quinsigamond Branch Library.

Worcester residents turned out en masse to welcome Prince Wilhelm of Sweden to the city on August 26, 1907. On that day, trolley cars throughout the city were bedecked with the royal coat of arms and crossed Swedish and American flags, as was every telephone pole lining the parade route. In the prince's honor, Swedish residents erected a 60-foot arch over Front Street, beneath which his cortège passed. The arch was a reproduction of the Norrebro Port, a 16th-century gate that had once been the north entrance to Stockholm's Gamla Stan. J.O. Emanuel Trotz pointed out to the royal visitor that Swedes had, "through honest work, ability, and integrity, . . . attained and envied a strong position among people from other lands who had settled in Worcester." This souvenir postcard shows both the arch and Prince Wilhelm greeting the cheering crowds.

Stig Lundquist, a popular local athlete, organized the Scandinavian Ski Club in November 1941. Between 1944 and 1952, annual competitions were held every February at the club's homemade ski slope on Newell Road in Holden. In this dramatic photograph, taken in the mid-1950s, a skier lifts off as the crowd watches intently. The view of the Bolton countryside is just as impressive.

After 1952, ski meets were held at other area sites, including Bolton. Here, we see members of the Scandinavian Ski Club lining the jump hill with snow, an arduous task indeed.

Victor and Julia Johnson hosted this 1916 Halloween gathering at their home for fellow members of the First Swedish Evangelical Congregational (Salem Square) Church.

The Swedish National Federation float makes its way up Main Street during the Worcester Centennial parade of 1948. For its efforts, the federation was awarded third prize for the most authentic folk costumes. To the far right, with his hands on his hips, is federation member William "Billy" Landquist.

Pastor Albert J. Laurell stands on the steps of the Lutheran Home for the Aged with Sister Lillie, house matron, and one of the home's residents in this c. 1950s photograph. Pastor Laurell did much to promote the area's Lutheran causes, which included organizing Auburn's Bethel Lutheran Church. The Swedish Lutheran old people's home on Harvard Street in Worcester was founded in 1920 to provide for the area's aging Swedish population. The home soon became an important institution, caring for non-Swedes and non-Lutherans as well. Enlarged over the years, it is today known as the Lutheran Home and is a testament to early Swedish benevolence.

J. Ernest Johnson, a member of the relay racing team of Kämpen Lodge No. 15 of the International Order of Good Templars, poses for a photograph c. 1920 at what looks like the lodge campgrounds on Sears Island in Worcester.

Ruby Dahlstrom (front) and Lillian Hohler serve newlyweds Kathleen (Grusell) and Carl Engvall at their 1950 wedding reception held at the International Order of Good Templars (IOGT) Hall on Ekman Street in Quinsigamond Village. This hall, constructed in 1892 by Quinsigamonds Väl Lodge of the International Order of Good Templars, became a gathering place for the neighborhood's numerous activities.

Shown here is a Midsummer celebration at Skogsblommen on Rotary Pond off Bylund Avenue in Auburn c. 1922. This location, with its clubhouse, was one of the icons of Swedish Auburn. Among those present are Magnus Bylund, Bror Bylund, Carl Carlson, and various Sundins, Nordstroms, Olsons, Pearsons, and Johnsons, along with a group of ladies from Boston.

The area's most distinguished Swedish-born politician, Republican Pehr Holmes appears here in a 1917 caricature. Holmes was born on the estate of Selma Lägerlöf in Mårbacka, Värmland, and came to Worcester at the age of four. He became mayor of Worcester, serving three terms (from 1917 to 1919) before becoming a member of the Governor's Council. In 1930, he was elected to Congress from the Fourth Congressional District, a position he retained until 1947.

Worcester was at the center of the 1940 presidential campaign when Republican candidate Wendell Willkie visited the city that fall. In this dramatic photograph, Congressman Pehr Holmes (center) listens to the candidate address the crowd from the back of his campaign train at Lincoln Square while Mrs. Willkie looks on. The radio reporter and loudspeakers add to the excitement of the moment.

J.A. (Johannes Alfred) Hultman, the so-called *solskenssångaren* (sunshine singer), was pastor of the Congregational church at Salem Square from 1900 to 1906. A fervent evangelical, the baritone was considered by many to be the top religious singer among Swedish-Americans. His concert tours included Europe and North America, and his song services at the Salem Square church drew packed houses of 1,200 or more. During a 1942 performance in California, he succumbed to a fatal heart attack while on stage.

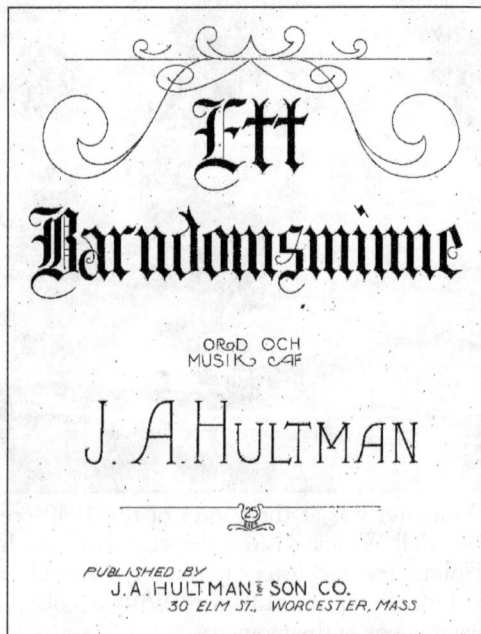

Shown here is a cover from a J.A. Hultman song sheet that was published in Worcester. Note his business address.

This remarkable 1888 photograph captures the scene of 36-year-old John Hanson's funeral in the newly established Swedish cemetery on Webster Street in Worcester. Hanson was brother to the first Swede recorded as entering Worcester, Carl "Charles" Hanson. All of the elements of an elaborate funeral are shown: the curious barefoot boys, the veiled women mourners at the top of the hill, the hearse with its driver in the rear, and the members of the Worcester Brass Band, of which Hanson was a member. The gravediggers on the left await the conclusion of Hanson's service. Hanson's fraternal brothers encircle their fellow member's coffin. (Courtesy of the Worcester Historical Museum.)

Prins Wilhelm föreläser på klingande svenska i Mechanics Hall i Worcester nästa söndag

e. m. kl. 3.15!!!

ETT EVENEMANG! FÖR WORCESTER ENDAST!

På allmän begäran av landsmän och landsmaninnor ges denna andra föreläsning i Worcester FÖR SVENSKAR EN-DAST och vidare TILL NEDSATT PRIS.

Biljetter till salu i morgon hos Lundborgs: $1.00, $1.50 och $2.00 samt om söndag vid ingången till Mechanics Hall.

PÅ KLINGANDE SVENSKA!

A notice appears in *Svea* announcing the arrival of Prince Wilhelm. The headline reads, "Prince Wilhelm will lecture in ringing Swedish in Mechanics Hall in Worcester next Sunday."

Prins Wilhelm sänder en hjärtlig hälsning till landsmännen i Worcester, för vilka han nästa onsdag föreläser

För tjugo år sedan hade jag den stora glädjen att besöka Er vackra stad. Det mottagande som svenskarna då beredde mig har djupt ristats i mitt minne. Jag gläder mig därför i dubbel måtto att återse den plats som gjort ett så outplånligt intryck och jag hoppas att om onsdag möta många gamla bekanta från den gången. Era landsmän därhemma skicka genom mig en hälsning till sina svenska fränder i Worcester. De veta att banden mellan Er och dem äro både starka och oslitliga. De glädja sig åt Edra framgångar, ty de veta att Ni göra det svenska namnet heder.

A greeting from Prince Wilhelm was sent to the Swedish people of Worcester prior to his arrival in January 1927. This was the second visit of the prince, who came and lectured on his experiences hunting big game on the African continent. The prince gave two talks—one in English, the other in Swedish.

Early on, the Salvation Army organized a Scandinavian corps that was active among the Worcester Swedish population. Two corps were formed—one in the heavily Swedish Quinsigamond Village and the second on Belmont Hill, another Swedish neighborhood. A campground was acquired in the early 1900s on Olga Avenue for summer preaching, conferences, and gatherings. Delegates to the Salvation Army Congress are gathered in this 1928 photograph.

These Salvation Army women are in a playful mood. Milé, Gerda, and friends enjoy a carefree moment in 1931.

The Höganäs Society held a picnic at the home of Carl and Sophie Ahlstrom on Glenwood Avenue in West Boylston during the summer of 1959. The host and hostess appear on the far left in the back row. Third from the left in the back row is Verner Nelson standing next to his wife, Norma, and beside them are Herbert Lundquist and his wife, Mae. The rest are unidentified.

The Scandinavian Women's Gymnastics Club is seen here on Midsummer's Day in 1920, shortly after its founding. The group had participated in this grandest of all Swedish festivals, which was held at the agricultural grounds in Greendale.

A postcard was sent out to attract attention to the forthcoming Swedish National Day and Midsummer Festival held at the agricultural grounds in Greendale on June 22, 1912. This particular celebration was one of the largest gatherings of area Swedes to date.

From its inception in 1923, the Scandinavian Athletic Club has supported a soccer league. The game was immensely popular among the Swedish immigrants, many of whom played on the SAC team. Shown here is a group of players c. 1925.

Although Sweden was officially neutral in World War II, Swedish-Americans were highly patriotic and showed their dedication to their adopted land. This September 1943 photograph shows members of the Swedish Folk Dance Club participating in a war bond rally at Worcester City Hall. The Swedish Folk Dance Club remained active in the Worcester area until the 1970s.

The John Ericsson Lodge No. 25 of the Vasa Order of America celebrates its 40th anniversary in 1940 with a banquet at the Hotel Bancroft in Worcester. It was once the largest Vasa lodge in the United States, with some 825 members. It still carries on, although with a much-reduced membership.

ACKNOWLEDGMENTS

The authors would like to thank the following people and organizations for helping to make this publication possible: Thurston and Shirley Solomon, Donald Bergdahl, Pete Petterson, Ida Sorblom, Astrid Grusell, Lee Ann Amend, C. Everett and Mrs. Holmes, Doris Veach, George Hultgren, Gladys Landquist, Ingrid Ward, Beverly Hobbs, Robert Haroian, Ture and Gloria Nilsson, Emma Lundquist, Steve and Jennifer Johnson, Dagny Johnson, Elaine Barrows, Sally Jablonski, Doris Johnson, Dawn Briggs, Dottie Rayla, Kay Sheldon, Vivian Lundquist, Howard Safstrom, Albert Peterson, Frances Johansen, Millie Johnson, Barbara (Johnson) Wilson, Susan Schonberg, Ken Ahlberg, Judith Crocker, Sven and Alice Carlson, Janet Sundquist, Amy Lindberg, Ruth Nordstrom, Helge Nordstrom, Crown Bakery, the Worcester Historical Museum, the Höganäs Museum, the Trinity Lutheran Church, the Belmont Street Baptist Church, the Bethel Lutheran Church, the Immanuel Lutheran Church, the Emanuel Lutheran Church, the Zion Lutheran Church, the Epworth United Methodist Church, the Quinsigamond United Methodist Church, the Chaffin Congregational Church, the Salem Covenant Church, the Scandinavian Athletic Club (SAC), and Lindquist and Lundin Funeral Home.

Lastly, thanks to Betty, Marilyn, and Tom for all of your patience, understanding, and encouragement during the preparation of this publication.

www.ingramcontent.com/pod-product-compliance
Lightning Source LLC
Chambersburg PA
CBHW050600110426
42813CB00008B/2412